T0171428

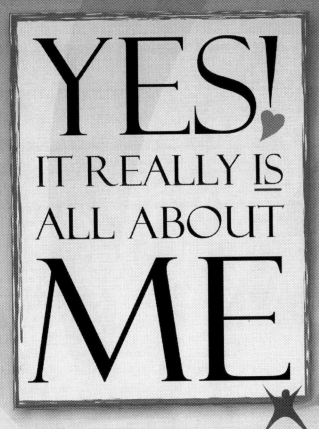

YES!
IT REALLY IS ALL ABOUT
ME

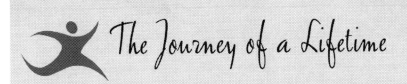

The Journey of a Lifetime

DARLEEN MILLER

Balboa Press books may be ordered through booksellers or by contacting:

Balboa Press
A Division of Hay House
1663 Liberty Drive
Bloomington, IN 47403
www.balboapress.com
1-(877) 407-4847

ISBN: 978-1-4525-3575-3 (sc)
ISBN: 978-1-4525-3576-0 (e)

Library of Congress Control Number: 2011909822

Printed in the United States of America

Balboa Press rev. date: 07/20/2011

Dedication

For all the selfless caregivers of the world
whose lives have been lovingly
devoted to serving others.

A special dedication to the family and friends
who have encouraged me throughout the years.

You have been my teachers, confidants,
and inspiration in my own journey of a lifetime.

This book is my labor of love.

1 HEARTBEAT

The heartbeat of life goes on and on...

Personal Information

Dear Reader: This is <u>your</u> journey of a lifetime; your opportunity to own and embrace the messages from your heart. Celebrate!

Name _____

Nickname _____

Age _____

Birthdate (mm/dd/yy) _____

Place of Birth _____

Current Address _____

Phone Number _____

Members of immediate family _____

Occupation _____

Contents

Preface

Yes! It Really IS All About Me is a self-empowerment journal creating community and support for infinite numbers of caregivers. It is a self-help 'inner-active' guide reflecting the wisdom of the heart. The diary format leads the reader in a step-by-step process of self-realization and self-nurturing, designed for the caregiver who loves others and wants to serve their world.

Each page asks specific questions to assist the reader in knowing their true self from a holistic body, mind, and spirit perspective. It is a journal that addresses aspects of the caregivers' life on many levels. After the question and answer there is a positive "I am" statement of healing.

This book can be used as a textbook within the context of a class or support group.

"Life can only be understood backwards; but it must be lived forwards." - Soren Kierkegaard

What is a Caregiver?

After years of experience, I define a caregiver as a healthcare provider, a person who cares for someone who is sick or disabled, an adult who cares for an infant or child, or any health professional. However, this term really applies to anyone who cares for another person, for example: parent, foster parent, sibling, child, teacher, babysitter, nanny, nurse, physician, salesperson, or social worker.

Rosalyn Carter defined it succinctly when she said, "There are only four kinds of people in the world – those who have been caregivers, those who are currently caregivers, those who will be caregivers, and those who will need caregivers."

My own definition of a caregiver encompasses the self. A caregiver supports and nurtures the needs of others and often neglects their own need for support and loving kindness.

Do any of these descriptions apply to you, the reader?

The number of caregivers in the medical community alone, has increased three times in the last five years and will continue to increase in the next ten. Currently, there are more than 65 million people in the United States alone who provide care for the chronically ill, disabled or aging family members or friends, and spend an average of 20 hours per week providing care for a loved one. This is 29% of our population, according to the National Alliance for Caregiving in collaboration with AARP (November 2009). An Evercare Survey, from the National Family Caregivers Association, documents that 47% of working caregivers report the increase in caregiving expenses has caused them to use all or most of their savings.

The impact on family caregivers health is startling as noted in the following statistics:

- 23% of family caregivers for loved ones report their health to be fair or poor.
- 55% skip their own doctor's appointments.
- 63% of caregivers report having poor eating habits and worsening exercise habits.
- 40% to 70% have clinically significant symptoms of depression; one-half of these caregivers meet the criteria for major depression.
- More than 1 in 10 (11% of family caregivers report that caregiving has caused their physical health to deteriorate).
- Family caregivers experiencing extreme stress have been shown to age prematurely taking approximately ten years off their lifespan.
- 83% of self-identified family caregivers believe their self-awareness led to increased confidence when talking to healthcare professionals about their loved ones' care.

Introduction

Yes! It Really IS All About Me will make an impact on the lives of caregivers. It will present a holistic perspective about nurturing the body, mind and spirit. Caregivers' happiness levels have declined and this book will create the opportunity to embrace life with enthusiasm and hope. As caregivers, we feel isolated, exhausted, stressed to the max, and are anxious and depressed. We feel that 'no one cares' and at times feel totally alone.

Caregivers need to learn how to play again each and every day. We are so busy nurturing others we forget about nurturing the self; we create selflessness. However, self-love is <u>not</u> selfish. We need to ask the question, "How can I nurture my soul, my intellect, my emotions, and my physical body? Caregivers matter in this world and we have been taught through parental and religious beliefs that 'it is better to give than to receive'. It is time for caregivers to develop their own personal 'To Do' list, which means we love and nurture ourselves as much as we love and nurture others in our lives.

Through my own lifetime experiences, I can relate to every one of the definitions of a caregiver. There were moments when exhaustion, anger, sorrow, fear and 'over-stressed' described my feelings. Indeed, there were days of depression and even resentment. It seemed like the 'To Do' lists never ended and there was very little time for my own well-being.

I thought I didn't have enough time to just cry and release all the pent-up emotions that kept building like a volcano. Silently inside, I was screaming to just take a few moments and stare into space or sit down without having to DO anything. The pangs of guilt were tugging at my heart and soul – "you <u>should</u> be doing this", or "you <u>should</u> be doing that". There was no one there to remind me to <u>STOP</u> 'should-ing' on myself.

The defining moment of my life appeared when I had ruptured a disc in my spine. It was time to make <u>big</u> changes in my choices as a human being. It was time to examine my life from a holistic mind-set. The whole person needed attention: my physical strength, my state of mind, my emotional and spiritual health. <u>I</u> was the only person that would be able to recognize my <u>own</u> nurturing and caregiving.

At that moment in time, I decided to pick myself up, dust myself off and begin to notice the value of my life on this planet. I was so busy taking care of the needs of others, I completely forgot about taking care of myself, too. However, now in my mind, taking care of the whole self is a practical choice for any survival program.

Life is swiftly changing for all of us. Change has and always will be a constant expression of living. Even though we want everything to remain the same, we cannot stop the process. So we think we have to work harder, be smarter, and give more to life to prevent the on-rushing changes in our lives. All of these actions become band-aids that shield us from reality.

Yes! It Really IS All About Me will open a new window to breathe the fresh air of existence and a new meaningful focus for all of us. It will help you discover your authentic self and your relationship to your own life. Embrace each moment of it with a new conscious awareness. Ask yourself, "what do I want to create?" because this is 'the journey of a lifetime'.

Who Am I?

Asking the question 'Who am I?" is answered by the statement "I am". A simple explanation of I AM is:

Intention

Awareness of your intention

Manifestation of your intention.

With awareness, we intend to manifest all things in our lives. All things have their own origin as energy. This is a magical life. We are becoming aware of our creative self, the feminine self which we all share. Understanding that we are all connected in an energy that allows us to live with a grateful heart is a conscious choice. We can lighten up our lives in joyfulness.

The time is now. Life is basically what I make it and it is ALL up to me. I am defining myself every waking moment. I may support the 'others' in my life, but I am walking in my OWN shoes. In that deep, quiet place, I know what is best for me.

Begin now to explore life from the inside out. Consider the following I AM affirmations: "I am becoming aware of me." This is the time to live in that awareness that will manifest and empower my relationship to myself and my relationship with the world. Be mindful that there is no one else in the world like you. "I am the sum total of all my experiences including the persons, places and things in my life." "I love that about myself because I am a unique creation and I am continuing to create every moment in my life." "I am making choices that ultimately affect me." "I am joyful in the rhythm of my own heart." "I am the genius that creates my own symphony. It is time for me to sing the song my heart was meant to sing." "I am the maestro of my life. My heart knows, my mind speaks to me with clarity." "I am awake now." "I am loving myself as much as I love and serve others."

The heartbeat of life goes on and on…..

1 HEARTBEAT

The heartbeat of life goes on and on...

House of PIES

The chapters are divided into four categories describing a holistic approach to an individual.
Physical,
Intellectual,
Emotional and
Spiritual components have been created to give the reader connection to the self.

Physical

Chapter One

Physical awareness includes connections of persons, places and things that create the tangible world in this present moment.

1. How would you describe your childhood?

....
....
....
....
....
....
....
....
....
....
....
....
....
....
....
....
....
....
....
....
....

 I am remembering my young life with respect and gratefulness.

2. What do you remember about your parents as a child?

....
....
....
....
....
....
....
....
....
....
....
....
....
....
....
....
....
....
....
....
....
....

 I am grateful for my parents and all the members of my immediate family.

3. Were you responsible for caregiving other members of your family at an early age?

....
....
....
....
....
....
....
....
....
....

Why?

....
....
....
....
....
....
....
....
....
....

I am respecting all caregivers, including myself.

4. What kinds of sports did you enjoy?

....

....

....

....

....

....

....

....

....

....

Why?

....

....

....

....

....

....

....

....

....

....

 *I am healthy and active.*

5. Did you have a mentor or coach for the sports you enjoyed? Explain.

....
....
....
....
....
....
....
....
....
....
....
....
....
....
....
....
....
....
....
....
....
....

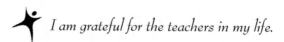 *I am grateful for the teachers in my life.*

6. Is there anything you would like to change if you could go back to your childhood and relive those days? Elaborate.

....
....
....
....
....
....
....
....
....
....
....
....
....
....
....
....
....
....
....
....
....

 *I am happy remembering my childhood.*

7. How were your grades? Were you an average student? Above average?

....
....
....
....
....
....
....
....
....
....
....
....
....
....
....
....
....
....
....
....
....
....

 I am accepting my academic childhood memories.

8. Were you expected to take care of siblings? Pets? Describe your earliest memories of caregiving them.

....
....
....
....
....
....
....
....
....
....
....
....
....
....
....
....
....
....
....
....
....
....

 *I am a natural caregiver.*

9. Did you have health issues as a child? If so, who was there to give you comfort and nurturance?

....
....
....
....
....
....
....
....
....
....
....
....
....
....
....
....
....
....
....
....
....

I am healthy and strong.

10. What activities gave you a sense of well-being? This could be anything, including the joy of school or a subject that touched your heart.

....
....
....
....
....
....
....
....
....
....
....
....
....
....
....
....
....
....
....
....
....
....

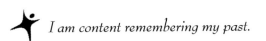 *I am content remembering my past.*

11. Who were the people that listened to you?

....
....
....
....
....
....
....
....
....
....

What were your feelings about them?

....
....
....
....
....
....
....
....
....
....

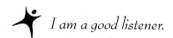 *I am a good listener.*

12. Where was your safe place? (reading, room, another person, etc.) Explain.

....
....
....
....
....
....
....
....
....
....
....
....
....
....
....
....
....
....
....
....
....
....
....
....

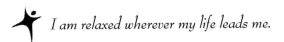 *I am relaxed wherever my life leads me.*

13. What were the expectations other people placed on you?

....
....
....
....
....
....
....
....
....
....
....
....
....
....
....
....
....
....
....
....
....

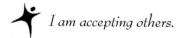 *I am accepting others.*

14. Who are your teachers/mentors in your adult life?

....

....

....

....

....

....

....

....

....

....

What were their roles?

....

....

....

....

....

....

....

....

....

....

....

....

....

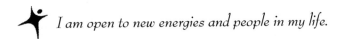 *I am open to new energies and people in my life.*

15. What are your favorite uplifting activities in life?

....
....
....
....
....
....
....
....
....
....

Why?

....
....
....
....
....
....
....
....
....
....
....

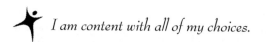 *I am content with all of my choices.*

16. Describe a special moment of rest and relaxation.

....

....

....

....

....

....

....

....

....

....

....

....

....

....

....

....

....

....

....

....

....

....

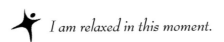 *I am relaxed in this moment.*

17. Do you enjoy traveling? Where and why?

....

....

....

....

....

....

....

....

....

....

....

....

....

....

....

....

....

....

....

....

 *I am interested in new places.*

18. Are you able to sleep peacefully?

....

....

....

....

....

....

....

....

....

....

....

Do you need medication to help you relax?

....

....

....

....

....

....

....

....

....

....

....

....

....

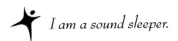 *I am a sound sleeper.*

19. What is your night-time routine?

 *I am relaxed at night.*

20. Do you take time out to go for a walk? If not, why?

....
....
....
....
....
....
....
....
....
....
....
....
....
....
....
....
....
....
....
....
....
....
....

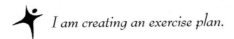 *I am creating an exercise plan.*

21. Do you enjoy physical exercise? What type do you enjoy?

....
....
....
....
....
....
....
....
....
....
....
....
....
....
....
....
....
....
....
....

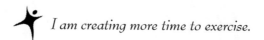 *I am creating more time to exercise.*

22. Are you happy with the job that you have? Explain.

....
....
....
....
....
....
....
....
....
....
....
....
....
....
....
....
....
....
....
....
....
....
....

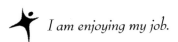 *I am enjoying my job.*

23. Where is home to you?

....
....
....
....
....
....
....
....
....
....

Why?

....
....
....
....
....
....
....
....
....
....

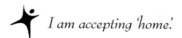 *I am accepting 'home.'*

24. Do you have a friend or group of friends you can call on for support?

....
....
....
....
....
....
....
....
....
....
....
....
....
....
....
....
....
....
....
....
....
....
....

 *I am creating larger groups of friends.*

25. What is your caregiver role?

....

....

....

....

....

....

....

....

....

....

....

....

....

....

....

....

....

....

....

....

....

....

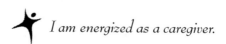 *I am energized as a caregiver.*

26. What is your daily routine?

....

....

....

....

....

....

....

....

....

....

....

....

....

....

....

....

....

....

....

....

....

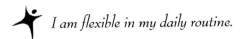 *I am flexible in my daily routine.*

27. What are those precious, joyful moments as
a caregiver? Be as specific as you can.

....

....

....

....

....

....

....

....

....

....

....

....

....

....

....

....

....

....

....

....

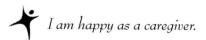 *I am happy as a caregiver.*

28. What are your prideful moments as a caregiver?

....
....
....
....
....
....
....
....
....
....
....
....
....
....
....
....
....
....
....
....
....

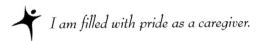 *I am filled with pride as a caregiver.*

29. Describe your health at this moment in time.

....
....
....
....
....
....
....
....
....
....
....
....
....
....
....
....
....
....
....
....
....

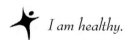 *I am healthy.*

30. In your caregiving position, how do you keep going?

....

....

....

....

....

....

....

....

....

....

....

....

....

....

....

....

....

....

....

....

....

 *I am observing my energy.*

31. What are your moments of celebration? Explain.

....

....

....

....

....

....

....

....

....

....

....

....

....

....

....

....

....

....

....

....

....

 *I am celebrating my life.*

32. Do you attend classes of any kind? What are the classes?

....
....
....
....
....
....
....
....
....
....

Why did you choose them?

....
....
....
....
....
....
....
....
....
....
....
....
....

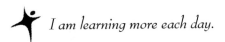 *I am learning more each day.*

33. Do you know Yoga or Tai Chi?

....
....
....
....
....
....
....
....
....
....

If yes, which one do you enjoy?

....
....
....
....
....
....
....
....
....
....

I am seeking a yoga class.

34. Describe your food regimen on a daily basis.
List foods and drink that give you comfort.

....

....

....

....

....

....

....

....

....

....

....

....

....

....

....

....

....

....

....

....

I am seeking a healthful diet.

35. What foods or drink agitate your energy?

....
....
....
....
....
....
....
....
....
....

Why?

....
....
....
....
....
....
....
....
....
....
....

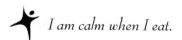 *I am calm when I eat.*

36. Does your economic situation cause you stress?

....
....
....
....
....
....
....
....
....
....

Why?

....
....
....
....
....
....
....
....
....
....

 I am releasing stress surrounding my economic situation.

37. Describe what activities give you peace of mind.

....
....
....
....
....
....
....
....
....
....

Why?

....
....
....
....
....
....
....
....
....
....
....

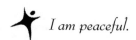 *I am peaceful.*

38. What else would be important to describe about your life? Right here, right now.

....
....
....
....
....
....
....
....
....

Why?

....
....
....
....
....
....
....
....
....
....
....
....
....

I am accepting my life, now.

39. What changes would you like to make in your life to give you hopefulness and joy?

....

....

....

....

....

....

....

....

....

Why?

....

....

....

....

....

....

....

....

....

....

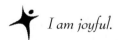 *I am joyful.*

40. Are you living up to someone else's expectations?

....
....
....
....
....
....
....
....
....
....

Are you happy with your choices?

....
....
....
....
....
....
....
....
....
....

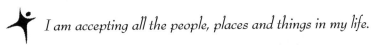 *I am accepting all the people, places and things in my life.*

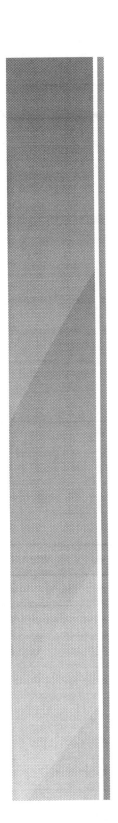

Intellectual

Chapter Two

This chapter relates to Intellectual choices of books and classes to expand the conscious mind.

1. Did you enjoy reading at an early age? What were your favorite books?

....
....
....
....
....
....
....
....
....
....

Why?

....
....
....
....
....
....
....
....
....
....

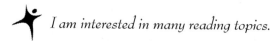 *I am interested in many reading topics.*

2. Did anyone read to you before bedtime?
   Describe a typical bedtime routine?

....
....
....
....
....
....
....
....
....
....
....
....
....
....
....
....
....
....
....
....
....
....

I am inspired to read.

3. What kinds of books do you enjoy reading today?

....

....

....

....

....

....

....

....

....

....

Why?

....

....

....

....

....

....

....

....

....

....

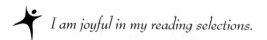 *I am joyful in my reading selections.*

4. What kinds of movies do you enjoy watching today?

....
....
....
....
....
....
....
....
....
....

Why?

....
....
....
....
....
....
....
....
....
....
....
....

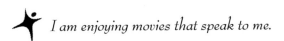 *I am enjoying movies that speak to me.*

5. What kinds of music do you enjoy?

....

....

....

....

....

....

....

....

....

....

Why?

....

....

....

....

....

....

....

....

....

....

....

 I am selecting categories of music that touch my heart.

6. What kinds of artwork inspire you?

....
....
....
....
....
....
....
....
....
....

Why?

....
....
....
....
....
....
....
....
....
....
....

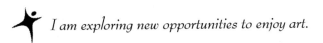 *I am exploring new opportunities to enjoy art.*

7. What kinds of classes were meaningful as a child?

....
....
....
....
....
....
....
....
....
....

Why?

....
....
....
....
....
....
....
....
....
....

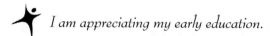 *I am appreciating my early education.*

8. What kinds of classes have you enjoyed as an adult (past and present)?

....
....
....
....
....
....
....
....
....
....

Why?

....
....
....
....
....
....
....
....
....
....
....
....
....

 I am selecting classes that meet my needs.

9. Did you consciously agree to your caregiving role?

....
....
....
....
....
....
....
....
....
....
....

Why?

....
....
....
....
....
....
....
....
....
....
....
....

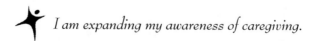 *I am expanding my awareness of caregiving.*

10. What are the 'shoulds' you impose on yourself?

....
....
....
....
....
....
....
....
....

Why?

....
....
....
....
....
....
....
....
....
....
....
....

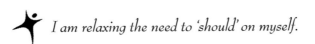 *I am relaxing the need to 'should' on myself.*

Emotional

Chapter Three

This chapter is devoted to the emotional impassioned connections to life.

1. Who gave you comfort when you were a child? Describe a time when you felt nurtured.

....
....
....
....
....
....
....
....
....
....
....
....
....
....
....
....
....
....
....
....
....
....
....

 *I am a reflection of my young life.*

2. Did you have a happy or unhappy school experience?

....
....
....
....
....
....
....
....
....
....

Explain.

....
....
....
....
....
....
....
....
....
....
....
....
....
....

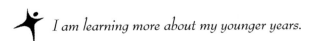 *I am learning more about my younger years.*

3. Who did you want to please in the family?

....
....
....
....
....
....
....
....
....
....

Why?

....
....
....
....
....
....
....
....
....
....

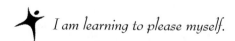 *I am learning to please myself.*

4. Did you feel accepted for the choices you made in your young life?

....

....

....

....

....

....

....

....

....

Why?

....

....

....

....

....

....

....

....

....

....

....

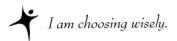 *I am choosing wisely.*

5. Did you have many friends in your young life?
If so, who were they and how did they treat you?

....
....
....
....
....
....
....
....
....

If few friends, did you feel moments of loneliness?

....
....
....
....
....
....
....
....
....
....
....
....

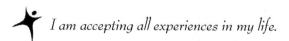 *I am accepting all experiences in my life.*

6. Did you ever have feelings of abandonment as a child?
   Describe any incident that created those feelings.

....
....
....
....
....
....
....
....
....
....
....
....
....
....
....
....
....
....
....
....
....
....

 *I am learning to love myself.*

7. Were you ever afraid as a child? Describe an event that created fear for you.

....

....

....

....

....

....

....

....

....

....

....

....

....

....

....

....

....

....

....

....

....

....

 *I am releasing all fears.*

8. Who was there to ease your pain or fear?

....
....
....
....
....
....
....
....
....
....

Describe their connection to you.

....
....
....
....
....
....
....
....
....
....
....
....

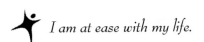 *I am at ease with my life.*

9. Describe a time when you felt total acceptance and love.

....

....

....

....

....

....

....

....

....

....

Did others play a role in your acceptance?

....

....

....

....

....

....

....

....

....

....

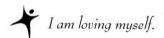 *I am loving myself.*

10. Who was there to share a special moment in your life?

....
....
....
....
....
....
....
....
....
....

Explain that moment.

....
....
....
....
....
....
....
....
....
....
....
....

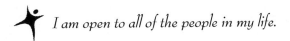 *I am open to all of the people in my life.*

11. Who helped you over the rough times in your life?

....

....

....

....

....

....

....

....

....

....

What were those difficult moments?

....

....

....

....

....

....

....

....

....

....

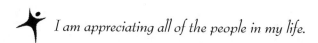 *I am appreciating all of the people in my life.*

12. Who or what gives you a feeling of contentment? Explain.

....

....

....

....

....

....

....

....

....

....

....

....

....

....

....

....

....

....

....

....

....

....

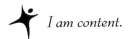 *I am content.*

13. Who was your support system as a child?
(mother, father, family, teachers, friends)

....

....

....

....

....

....

....

....

....

....

....

....

....

....

....

....

....

....

....

....

....

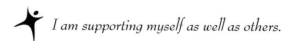 *I am supporting myself as well as others.*

14. What was a big disappointment in your life?

....
....
....
....
....
....
....
....
....

Why?

....
....
....
....
....
....
....
....
....
....
....
....

 *I am emotionally content.*

15. Did you ever feel betrayed by anyone? How did you handle that betrayal?

....
....
....
....
....
....
....
....
....
....
....
....
....
....
....
....
....
....
....
....
....

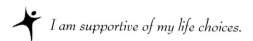 *I am supportive of my life choices.*

16. Who helped create joy in your life?

....
....
....
....
....
....
....
....
....
....

Describe a situation when you felt joyful.

....
....
....
....
....
....
....
....
....
....
....
....
....

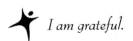 *I am grateful.*

17. Did you ever have feelings of not being good enough?

....
....
....
....
....
....
....
....
....
....

Describe a situation.

....
....
....
....
....
....
....
....
....
....
....
....

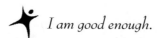 *I am good enough.*

18. Are you a perfectionist? Explain your answer.

....

....

....

....

....

....

....

....

....

....

....

....

....

....

....

....

....

....

....

....

....

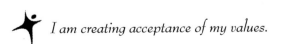 *I am creating acceptance of my values.*

19. Did you ever feel tired of taking care of other people? Explain a situation.

....
....
....
....
....
....
....
....
....
....
....
....
....
....
....
....
....
....
....
....
....
....

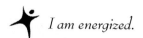 *I am energized.*

20. What is an embarrassment to you?

....
....
....
....
....
....
....
....
....
....

Why?

....
....
....
....
....
....
....
....
....
....
....
....
....

I am embracing my life.

21. Who or what makes you laugh?

....

....

....

....

....

....

....

....

....

....

Why?

....

....

....

....

....

....

....

....

....

....

....

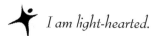 *I am light-hearted.*

22. How does a sunset make you feel?

....
....
....
....
....
....
....
....
....
....
....
....
....
....
....
....
....
....
....
....
....
....

I am appreciating the beauty of the Earth.

23. Is your life fast-paced? Explain.

....

....

....

....

....

....

....

....

....

....

....

....

....

....

....

....

....

....

....

....

....

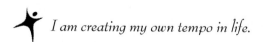 *I am creating my own tempo in life.*

24. Where do you go for peace and quiet? Explain.

....
....
....
....
....
....
....
....
....

Why?

....
....
....
....
....
....
....
....
....
....
....
....

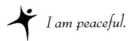 *I am peaceful.*

25. How do you handle changes in your life?

....
....
....
....
....
....
....
....
....
....
....
....
....
....
....
....
....
....
....
....
....
....

 *I am embracing newness in life.*

26. Why do you avoid certain people in your life?

....

....

....

....

....

....

....

....

....

....

....

....

....

....

....

....

....

....

....

....

....

....

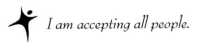 *I am accepting all people.*

27. Are there people in your life who like to argue?
What is your energy like when you argue?

....
....
....
....
....
....
....
....
....
....
....
....
....
....
....
....
....
....
....
....

I am creating new viewpoints.

28. Are you able to confront those argumentative people? Do you find yourself at a loss for words when talking to others you believe to be stronger than you?

....
....
....
....
....
....
....
....
....
....
....
....
....
....
....
....
....
....
....
....
....
....
....

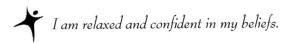 *I am relaxed and confident in my beliefs.*

29. Do you enjoy gossiping with your friends?

....
....
....
....
....
....
....
....
....
....

Why?

....
....
....
....
....
....
....
....
....
....
....

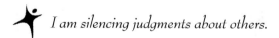 *I am silencing judgments about others.*

30. Do you make judgments about other people?

....

....

....

....

....

....

....

....

....

....

List expectations you have about them.

....

....

....

....

....

....

....

....

....

....

....

....

....

 *I am in harmony with myself.*

31. Do you ever feel anger at people in your life?

....

....

....

....

....

....

....

....

....

....

Why?

....

....

....

....

....

....

....

....

....

....

 I am okay, knowing my anger is appropriate.

32. How do you resolve your angry feelings?

....
....
....
....
....
....
....
....
....

How do you handle your emotions when confronting others?

....
....
....
....
....
....
....
....
....
....

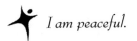 *I am peaceful.*

33. Do you feel there is enough time for **you** in your life?

....

....

....

....

....

....

....

....

....

....

....

....

....

....

....

....

....

....

....

....

....

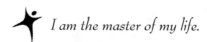 *I am the master of my life.*

34. Do you feel stressed and overwhelmed most of the time? Why?

....
....
....
....
....
....
....
....
....
....
....
....
....
....
....
....
....
....
....
....
....
....
....

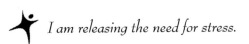 *I am releasing the need for stress.*

35. Are you fearful about your future? Give details.

....
....
....
....
....
....
....
....
....
....
....
....
....
....
....
....
....
....
....
....
....
....

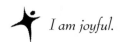 *I am joyful.*

36. Who gives you compassion and recognition for who you are?

....
....
....
....
....
....
....
....
....
....
....
....
....
....
....
....
....
....
....
....
....
....

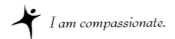 *I am compassionate.*

37. How do you feel about holidays?
Do you have happy memories of past holidays?

....

....

....

....

....

....

....

....

....

Explain.

....

....

....

....

....

....

....

....

....

....

 I am feeling optimism about the holidays.

Spiritual

Chapter Four

This chapter is about our connection to the unseen energy we call spirit.

1. Who are you — really?

....
....
....
....
....
....
....
....
....
....

Why?

....
....
....
....
....
....
....
....
....
....

 *I am an ongoing work in progress.*

2. What books have you read to support your curiosity about your spiritual development?

....
....
....
....
....
....
....
....
....
....
....
....
....
....
....
....
....
....
....
....
....
....
....

 I am confident in my choices to grow and evolve in this lifetime.

3. What is your grandest dream?

....
....
....
....
....
....
....
....
....
....

When did you recognize your dream?

....
....
....
....
....
....
....
....
....
....

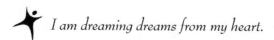 *I am dreaming dreams from my heart.*

4. What are the peaceful moments in your life?

....
....
....
....
....
....
....
....
....
....
....
....
....
....
....
....
....
....
....
....
....
....
....
....

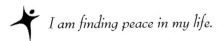 *I am finding peace in my life.*

5. What gifts and talents do you remember from your childhood?

....
....
....
....
....
....
....
....
....
....

When did you recognize your gifts and talents?

....
....
....
....
....
....
....
....
....
....

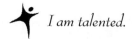 *I am talented.*

6. What were some of your hopes and dreams as you
grew and began to seek options for your future?

....
....
....
....
....
....
....
....
....
....
....
....
....
....
....
....
....
....
....
....
....

I am embracing my hopes and dreams.

7. Do you believe you have a purpose in life?

....

....

....

....

....

....

....

....

....

....

If yes, what is it?

....

....

....

....

....

....

....

....

....

....

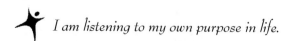 *I am listening to my own purpose in life.*

8. Do you meditate? If not, would you like to learn meditation as a technique for relaxation?

....
....
....
....
....
....
....
....
....
....
....
....
....
....
....
....
....
....
....
....
....
....

 *I am relaxed and connected to Universal Energy.*

9. Do you rely on your belief system?
   What beliefs give you comfort?

....

....

....

....

....

....

....

....

....

....

....

....

....

....

....

....

....

....

....

....

....

 *I am comforted by my belief in me.*

10. Do you appreciate your life?

....
....
....
....
....
....
....
....
....
....

Why?

....
....
....
....
....
....
....
....
....
....
....
....
....
....

I am appreciating my life because I am AWESOME!

About the Author

"You must not let your life run in the ordinary way. Do something that no one else has done, something that will dazzle the world. Show that God's creative principle works in you." – Paramahansa Yogananda

In what seems like a lifetime ago, Darleen Miller became an ongoing student of life. Growing up, her three-generational family were living and surviving together in a single dwelling. As a result of this, she observed the many complications of war, loss, grief, economic adversity, abandonment, disappointment and caretaking that were present on an ongoing basis.

As an only child, she created her own world of survival through sports, including softball, tennis, basketball and would you believe, football?

Her mother, as the sole breadwinner in the family, demanded excellent grades from Darleens' scholastic choices. She also demanded 'perfection' and an 'A' average, which were normal requirements for Darleen. Stress and anguish began to build in massive proportions. In those formative years, Darleen realized she was expected to be her Mother's keeper. She was the 'go to' energy that nurtured her mom.

The two activities of spiritual studies and regular church attendance brought great solace and joy to Darleen. Come rain or shine, Darleen spent Sunday in church listening to the sermons, listening to her mother sing, and sometimes, even sleeping in one of the pews.

As a degreed teacher, Darleen continued her quest for more knowledge with post-graduate courses in English, Psychology, Music and Spirituality. With every passing year, family and friends encouraged her to "write a book". Her dreams went largely unrealized with the exception of winning an Outstanding Achievement Award from the International Society of Poets for her published poem, "Universal Hope". This award was the motivation to review the many handwritten spiral notebooks, diaries and countless flip charts used as teaching tools from her many classes. Holistic training gave Darleen a solid foundation of living one day at a time and knowing the dawn of her ambition would be near. She never gave up hope.

As a dedicated, holistic teacher of children and adults, Darleen was also a military wife of 20 years. She cared for her husband and family in times of crisis, economic downturn, and personal loss. With three ambitious, gifted and talented children, there was little time to 'stop and smell the roses'. Being a caregiver most of her life, Darleen always put her own need for nurturing on hold.

Caregiving responsibilities expanded with her aging, seriously ill parents, together with caring for her husband who endured heart disease, diabetes and cancer, which ultimately claimed his life in July of 2010.

"This is the moment of realization," comments Darleen, as she establishes a platform through writing a book and teaching about a subject near and dear to her heart. The labor-of-love book – *Yes! It Really IS All About Me* has been years in creation. The book is a step-by-step guide for everyone who has been, or who is now, a caregiver.

In the caregiver's belief system, it is perceived that, "someone else and their needs are more important than my own". *Yes! It Really IS All About Me* will guide all of us to examine our own thoughts and emotions which in turn will bring a light to each heart. It will offer a ray of sunshine to all caregivers from all walks of life.

With new energy realizations in this 21st Century, Darleen believes it is each person's destiny to take care of the heart that beats for others. In her own words, "I have something to contribute via all of my life experiences. They molded my life into the visionary I am today. I view the past with love and respect and I envision the future with hopeful anticipation. All can view their lives as a star in their own universe and live one day at a time with a loving awareness of their own gifts and talents."

"Sing the song your heart was meant to sing." - Darleen Miller

Author Qualifications

Master Energy Healer (Reiki)
Teacher
Author
Visionary

Teaching: The following is a list of Classes and/or Workshops taught and offered for beginners, intermediate and advanced healing practitioners:

Ayurvedic Principles
Deep Relaxation
Meditation
Breathing Exercises
Energy Awareness
Cleansing Techniques
I AM Technique
Kundalini Yoga
Body/Mind Massage
Reconnective Healing
Evolutionary Reiki (ER)
Transcendence Technique
Sound and Vibrational Healing

Philosophy: My heart path has always been focused on guiding individuals and groups to start the journey toward understanding and knowingness about the age-old questions – Who am I? and Why am I here? Ultimately, there is no energetic separation of the spirit, mind and body. We all have a divine relationship with the self.

Influential teachers who have inspired me to view life from an expanded consciousness:

Influential Teachers: Caroline Myss
Wayne Dyer
Depak Chopra
Dr. Norman Sheely
Dr. Eric Pearl
Jean Houston
Karunamai
Mother Meera
Brian Weiss
James Van Prague
Barbara DeAngelis
Aleta St. James
Eckhart Tolle
Mitchell Gaynor
Napoleon Hill

Personal Pages

for Expanded Thoughts
and Heartbeats

I am living each moment of my life in love.

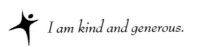 *I am kind and generous.*

I am celebrating my life.

....

....

....

....

....

....

....

....

....

....

....

....

....

....

....

....

....

....

....

....

....

....

....

....

....

....

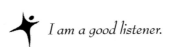 *I am a good listener.*

When will the mirror reflect who I am inside?